COME SOOTHE MY SOUL

Inspiration to encourage and support life growth

A nourishing thought provoking companion of poetry, prose and views to inspire and encourage the spirit

By

juanita parker

© 2003 by juanita parker. All rights reserved.

No part of this book may be reproduced, stored in a retrieval system, or transmitted by any means, electronic, mechanical, photocopying, recording, or otherwise, without written permission from the author.

ISBN: 0-7596-5229-5 (e-book)
ISBN: 0-7596-5230-9 (Paperback)
ISBN: 0-7596-5231-7 (Hardcover)

This book is printed on acid free paper.

Scripture taken from the New King James Version. Copyright © 1982 by Thomas Nelson, Inc. Used by permission. All rights reserved.

1stBooks – rev. 02/04/03

Dedicated to:

Mom, J. Cleophia Parker
and
my son, Charles D. Florence

In memory of family
vessels of creativity:
Dad: Willie Parker [1920–1996]
Grandfather: Henry Carroll [1884–1973]
Grandmother: Bertha Brown Carroll [1884-1972]

Acknowledgements

My heartfelt love and gratitude to my special group of prayer partners and friends who took the time to listen, read and encourage me to complete this work:

To Darlene Pachót, Lynda Holmes, Paulette Barńe, Linda Allen and Jackie Terry, thank you for hanging together in our sessions for more than a year to encourage, inspire and motivate one another to move forward in our life purposes, visions and dreams. It's working!

Gail Stephen, thank you for being the innovative net-worker, communicator, supporter and friend in helping to complete some major details.

Sylvia Collier, thank you for your editing assistance, enthusiasm and encouragement.

Tina Allen, thank you for your constant support, encouragement, sharing and uplifting my spirit with love and humor. Your commitment and perseverance to your art and craft inspired my tribute to you entitled *Tina Allen, You Are Distinctively...*.

Thank you Darlene, it is always a pleasure to sit and talk with you as seconds and minutes turn into hours, because we can't stop talking about the goodness of the Lord in our lives. You are my spiritual sister, friend, and a wonderful encourager. I thank God for you and your husband, Tony. Thank you Tony Pachót for putting up with Darlene and me during our long visits and telephone conversations.

David Rice, thank you for taking time from your busy schedule to correspond, share and encourage me in this process. May the end result—this poetic book in your hand—bring to you tremendous inspiration.

Terri McFaddin we've been friends so long that I was inspired to write *Ode To My Friend*, just for you, so somebody can help us recollect how we met in case we happen upon senility. Thanks for your encouragement and sharing recreational, have-a-ball, splurge times!

To Roz, Ashley and Theresa, my favorite girls. It is so wonderful to know that I have inspired and mentored you in some way that is rewarding to your lives. You are purpose-full, destined by God.

To Janet Bailey, Gailey Ward, Dr. Shahida Phiri, Paula Loeb, Mary Osby and Henrietta Davis – Thank you for being gracious ladies. It's great when we are together socially – shopp'n—eat'n—talk'n—travel'n—sing'n—shout'n – I've learned much from you!

To my mom, Mrs. J. C. Parker, I dedicate these first writings to you, introducing another side of me that is enhanced by some of your creative sense of humor that helps to balance out my sometimes overwhelming seriousness. Hope you enjoy it—and if you don't—don't worry, I'm writing another one!

Desmond, my son; May God grant you the desires of your heart as you cultivate your path. Always put God in the forefront and take wisdom, knowledge and understanding as assets to help accomplish your goals. I love you!

Dr. E. V. Hill, thank you for preaching and teaching a stable gospel from the Word of God that has enriched and empowered the lives of us who physically, spiritually and mentally grew up at Mt. Zion Missionary Baptist Church under your leadership. Thank you for inspiring my life. You will always be, Pastor.

To Bishop Noel Jones, thank you for the continuous encouragement I receive through your invigorating sermons that have challenged me to move to another level in this season. I have gained much from your teaching and preaching ministry. I truly, have had, a soul revival.

Because all of you are so very special to me, there is a tribute to you entitled *Supportive People.* Much love and blessings.

How To Utilize This Book

Come Soothe My Soul is designed for personal and group use. It is a companion that will provide inspiration, encouragement and laughter along with the opportunity to revitalize the inner spirit. A Prayer of Thanksgiving page is provided to help focus and invigorate your spiritual expressions and thoughts. You can make that page personal by writing a brief sentence prayer, praise and/or confirmation of your own.

For enjoyment read a poem or vignette through, then go back and put your own rhythmic beat to each stanza. Stand up and read it out loud with expression and motion. Swing those hands, move that head, shake that body, if necessary. You may experience a sense of relief from stress as you stir up and release energy from within. There is rhythm and motion in everything that we do.

Getting together with friends for a poetry reading session is another way to use *Come Soothe My Soul*. The poetry and prose provides opportunities for dialogue on different subject matter, giving room to share heart-to-heart communication, interpretation, reflection and expression with those participating.

I suggest a tea party with friends, a book club meeting or create an atmosphere for an evening tête-à-tête perhaps by candlelight, a lovely fireplace or round-table setting. Be creative. As you read through different lines, find subject matter that will enhance communication and conversation. Surprisingly, your guests will leave refreshed and inspired. Whatever you choose to do, just enjoy it!

Introduction

As a child, coming from a small family of four—dad, mom, my brother and me—I had lots of quiet time to spend creatively. Every evening when my mother and father would return home from work, our daily evening ritual was to sit at the kitchen table to have dinner together. As we enjoyed our delicious food and conversation, we would reflect over our day, our studies and work, which usually concluded with laughter and jokes. Sometimes we talked a lot, and sometimes we just sat and ate quietly. The important thing was the unity and harmony shared during dinner time helped to create and strengthen our family bond with stability and love.

When alone, I would write down my thoughts and make up stories. That's how I kept myself company when my brother and I were not playing checkers, Monopoly or roller-skating.

In later years, I had a playmate who likewise had a gift for making up interesting stories. Together we were two adolescent girls living in the center of our imaginative worlds trying to out-do one another with our original poems and stories. Many times we were so absorbed in our episodes that we ignored the fact that we were walking each other back and forth home more than twice in the same day. We had a narrative for anything that got our attention: people in the neighborhood, trees, cars, it did not matter as long as we had a subject to construct a story. We enjoyed creating and sharing our thoughts with each other.

Outside of my voracious desire to glean from the mind, where did my desire to write come from? I consider it a gift from God, but I discovered that this gift has been in my family for generations.

One day, while searching through some old papers my mother gave me, I came across an allegory my grandfather had handwritten. It was well written and thought provoking. My mother said my grandfather used to write essays and allegories for church programs, and my grandmother, as the orator, would read them during her presentations. My mother likewise has a witty sense of poetic style. On many occasions she has written mind-boggling riddles and clues to assist me in finding my hidden birthday presents. She still does that to this very day. Oh, my!

Now, we have entered into a phase of life where chaos parades with rave reviews, revealing serious drama. Life's affairs are challenging, confusing and overwhelming at times. In our fast-paced society, we find that we have more issues and circumstances to deal with than ever before. Striving to achieve a meaningful and fulfilled life, we work hard to keep ourselves together in order to deal with the changes that we go through. Many times this may present a challenge to transform the way we think, act, and project ourselves in order to overcome the unexpected or expected results.

Life dictates so many stressful situations that in order to successfully make it through, we must learn how to discipline and train ourselves in the art of composure and flexibility in order to keep from flipping out or forfeiting our mission and positive contribution to society.

So you say to yourself—I'm going to sit down and think of a new direction and undertake a new challenge—only to make a new discovery about yourself, that you have a need to get in touch with yourself and to retreat from the trials of the world. So you look for a comfortable seat where you can relax. While trying to sit still for a moment in silence, you recognize that the world does not offer the kind of serenity and peace that you need; so you close your eyes and begin to search from within for a safe place. That's when you discover a higher authority is there to meet you, comfort you, and to calm your mind, body and soul.

As you read the enclosed lines of thoughts and inspiration, I hope you find something written that will satisfy your inner being, especially knowing that along with you, someone else is progressing through life with hope and expectation in spite of the devastation, odds, or whatever the stops and detours are that this journey may bring.

There is a guide within that helps us to triumph over and beyond those rubber bands that appear to cause a vacillating reaction. So relax, and go to the source that is higher. Take a moment to breathe the breath of life, and soothe your soul.

    Love, kindness and peace be with you –
    Juanita Parker

Table Of Contents

How To Utilize This Book vii

Introduction ix

Dedication 1

Birds Sing At Midnight 3

Looking Back 6

The Harvest 8

Oh, Why Me? 10

Change 13

Come Soothe My Soul 15

Lessons Learned 19

Closure 21

Cocoon 23

Destination 25

Elevate 27

Abandonment 29

Been There – May Go Again 31

Arrival 33

Solitude 35

Image 38

Pondering Thoughts 40

Ode To My Friend, Terri	43
Ode To My Hair	46
Ode To The DJ	48
Power In The Name Of Jesus	50
Revival	52
I. The Situation	52
II. Stillness	53
III. Requests	54
IV. Inquiry	55
V. Assurance	56
VI. Testimony	57
VII. Answer	58
VIII. Rejoice	59
VX. Revived	60
Direction	62
Tool For The Mission	64
Alter Call	66
Seasons	69
Trials and Tribulations	71
The Quest Of Love	73
Jubilance	76
The Power Of Fear	78
Transition	80
Creativity	82

Inspiration	85
Melodic Motion	87
Light	89
Enslaved	91
Energy	94
Bravery	96
Panic Attack	98
Three Requests	100
Supportive People	102
Valuable Woman	104
Communing With God	106
Diligence	107
Trust	109
Today	111
Instant Replay	113
The Miracle Of Voice Tones	115
Tina Allen, You Are Distinctively…	117
The Creed Of A Wise Woman	119
Nurturing	122
Today, I Think I Met Him	125
Experience	128
Assurance	132

Vision 134

The High Road 136

Dedication

I call Him Lord because He is my ultimate teacher
I call Him King because He is the head of my life
I call Him Father because of His love towards me
I call Him Ruler because He knows how, when and where to direct my path
I call Him—

I call Him Faithful because He keeps the promises He has made to me
I call Him Committed because He is always devoted to me
I call Him—

I call Him Keeper because He watches over me so tenderly
I call Him Savior because He purchased my salvation to set me free
I call Him Counselor because when I'm troubled He gives me solutions
I call Him—

I call Him Almighty because when I'm weak
it is His strength that makes me strong
I call Him Deliverer because when in bondage
He revives my soul
I call Him—

I call Him God because He created everything
I call Him Sovereign because He reigns supreme
I call Him Compassionate because He is full of mercy and grace
I call Him a Burning Fire because His Spirit lives within my soul
I call Him anytime, anywhere and He hears my cry
I call Him –
He is the Creator of life

juanita parker

Oh Mighty God, you are matchless in all creation. You are greater than space and time. Great is your spirit within me and your mercy towards me. I honor you for who you are, Almighty living God. I give you praise.

For this God is our God for ever and ever: he will be our guide even unto death. Psalms 48:14

Come Soothe My Soul

Birds Sing At Midnight

I was playing the piano
one warm summer evening
entranced by a melody,
the room was still
music filled the air
when I heard a bird singing
from—somewhere

The bird's trilling tweets serenaded the wind,
the limb of a tree was her stage
the more I played
the more she sang
I truly became her competition

I wondered
if she would ever stop,
and just—fly away,
but the more she sang
the less I played
and tuned my ears to listen

From the east bay window
I could see an orange fireball
blazing in the sky
as the bird's rhythm
became challenging
I could hardly close my eyes

That's when I picked up a pen
and some paper
to appease and
console my mind

The songs in the night
were so clearly defined
not a single thought was
blurry –

juanita parker

I began to retreat
to the birds rapid beat
as she expressed a melodic story
when suddenly the bird flew away
and I went to sleep humming
the melody she sang
at midnight
somewhere around
early morning

Come Soothe My Soul

Thank you Lord for reminding me that in my restlessness you are present. Thank you for cheering my spirit and consoling my heart, showing me continuously that you are the peace who comforts me at all times. For this, I give you praise.

juanita parker

Looking Back

looking back wondering
if the choices you made
were the substance of your mistakes

looking back to peek at the things
that displeased you
but you accepted them anyway

looking back to sense
the hurt and pain that you think
people caused you

looking back to pick up
pieces of broken dreams
trying to make them a reality

isn't it time to let go?
you know
it's never too late
to move forward
so why bother looking back
holding onto the past

welcome what remained
a wealth of experience
to carry you through
the atmosphere of change

a new look at life
a new view in sight
moves you toward
the crystal light
producing for you, clear vision

Thank you Lord for the wealth of experiences, whether good or bad, that have helped to grow and develop my character to this point, and taught me to look forward with vision and hope. I am forever, grateful.

juanita parker

The Harvest

there are times
when the web of life
will engulf you on every hand
times when everything will go wrong
manipulating your life's goals and plans

that's the time to release your courage
to contend with all you've got
by letting nothing distress your spirit
and take you off your course

the ground you seek is fertile
for planting seeds today
the process is full of struggles
as you put action into play

however, tomorrow will bring the harvest
an inheritance from the growth
an abundant wealth of knowledge
and wisdom
to distribute the treasure's oath

the harvest will seek you out
with bountiful giving hands
returning to you double portions,
abundant favor, and prosperity
to spread throughout the land

Thank you Lord for guiding me safely through the dark tunnels of my insight and lack of understanding. Thank you for illuminating my mind through your Word, and changing my desires so I can be a productive vessel. All praises.

juanita parker

Oh, Why Me?

Something happened you didn't like
so now you sit in a corner
blundering and brawling;
your attitude is really hot.
Somebody just mistreated you, and
You want to get "them" back.

You are so caught up in the moment
your anger's hit high altitude
You can't even see
The devil's little workers
Trying to sabotage you.

Sure, you want everyone to love you
And what you're doing all at the same time
But not everyone is going to embrace you
Some are the envious and jealous kind.

As a matter of fact, the very moment you feel like
You're on top of the world
Someone's got a discouraging word
that causes you to yield to temptation.

Worst yet, you can be at your highest degree in spirit
dealing with what you know to be right –
you were minding your own business when suddenly somebody
called you the bad guy
– they just did not understand, you.

One moment to triumph, please?
Catch a hold of yourself and shake up your mind.
Just a reminder, you have a supernatural source to turn to – That is a fact, not just a thought.

You can't see the hands working on your behalf: They are invisible.
Remember, God is a Spirit.
When you call on Him in prayer,
perhaps an angel will come to your rescue

so you can get out of the dumps,
out of the corner brawling,
prepared for the next battle.

Oh, why me?
Rest assured,
God is in total control
of your situation.

juanita parker

Thank you Lord for teaching me to bridle my tongue and lift my mind beyond what I hear, think and see. I ask for continuous wisdom to resist the darts of my enemies visible or invisible, in spirit and mind. Thank you for surrounding me with heavenly hosts to fight my battles. I exalt you, Hallelujah.

Change

you say you want to change
but you continue in the same direction
doing the same unworkable things
that end only in disaster

you say you want to live your purpose
but your biggest defeat is you

you say you have visions and dreams
yeah, you live to fulfill them too
yet you ignore the obvious
when the door is opened for you

you say everything must be in order
you need the time to do it
but you refuse to believe in the invisible source
faith is required of you

There is power working on your behalf
if you will to believe
one step triggers the path
mixed with the influence of
focused sight and faith
follow the trail
perform on the path
sooner than you think
it will be
visual reality

juanita parker

Thank you Lord for keeping me from self-destruction for there are times that I am my own worst enemy. Thank you for the steps that you ordered for me to walk in today. Thank you for faith and belief.

Come Soothe My Soul

in the silhouette of the morning dawn
i awakened
as the Spirit of the Lord nudged my being
the taunts of my wounded soul
kept coming forth
seeking relief

i turned on the radio
searching for a Word
to calm my disdainful thoughts
the messenger recited the word,
the word was faith

i listened
and with haste
turned off the radio

in the quietness of the morning
i sought after answers
something to soothe my soul

i was thinking on the circumstances
that caused my discomfort
while my eyes were filled with tears
the controlling factors of my distress
my tarnished armor
caused me unrest

as i talked to the Lord
about the particulars of my pain
i felt wounded
used
unappreciated, abused
skeletons of human imperfection
seeking clarity

juanita parker

somewhere
out of nowhere
in the depths of the room

over the darkness and the gloom
i heard screeching words ring out
"closure,
it is time for closure"

the pound of my soul
pulsated within
i could not conquer the trials
of my path
until i learned how to forgive

in my search for relief
a soft inner voice
firmly spoke reminding me that
i am called
anointed
chosen by God
to employ His perfect plan

that's my life

i must take my eyes off of what i see
feel and hear
abandon all negative responses
all of my trust
i place in God
while the enemy's plot is to sift me

i must tighten up my armor
sharpen up my sword
with confidence i will continue

God forgives and forgets

so must i

Come Soothe My Soul

while i struggle in the battle of life
there are times i must retreat
to a secret place
to be revived
to be renewed
to receive my Commander's instructions

in his presence
a comforting place
i know he will revive me again
as he comes to soothe my soul with rest
and bestow upon me the gift of
peace

juanita parker

Thank you Lord for your refreshing presence. Thank you for your loving spirit. Thank you for a quiet place to retreat. Thank you for communing with me and giving me instructions so I can get back up and continue.

Lessons Learned

While God gives strength to endure the most difficult challenges, the lessons learned from the struggles produce strength bonded with experience. For some will rave over your good works, while others will tear you down. Even then, remember to stand with humility if abusive words and witty remarks are verbalized to demean your character, for power comes when you refuse to retaliate --
even when talked about,
even when disliked;
even when prejudged,
even when people who don't know anything about you assume they do.

It is good to follow God's lead,
no matter what others may think or say,
just take to heart these words of assurance,
God is all that you need and all that you need
God is.
In his image you are created,
so who knows better what is best for you
than the one who made you?

juanita parker

Thank you Lord for the challenges in my life that extend lessons, reveal knowledge and provide wisdom so I can expand with love. Teach me how not to judge others as they have judged or mistreated me. Create in me a forgiving heart and a forgetful mind of the offenses.

Closure

At the dawn of morning, I prayed and praised God:

Forgive me Lord for falling into the pits of hellish thoughts.

Forgive me Lord for taking my mind off the knowledge and wisdom in your Word.

Forgive me for falling into the traps of the enemy.

Give me a forgiving heart and a forgetful mind for the aggressions of others who were placed to hinder and delay me.
I want to go forward.

Thank you Lord.
In the name of Jesus. – Amen

I waited on the Lord.

Thereafter, His voice pierced my mind with clarity.
How much more did I understand his call.

Yes, there are questions, and God has all the answers.
I feel better because I know that He is leading me, pulling me, shifting me.
His answers may not always be what I want to hear,
but His answers are always right.

God is the solution to my situation.
I have the assurance that everything is going to be all right.
When He answered my prayer,
I felt safe,
I felt peace,
I felt comfort
as I went back to sleep –
I found closure.

juanita parker

Thank you Lord for forgiving me of my sins and teaching me how to forgive myself and to forgive others who have unjustly mistreated me. Thank you for clearing my heart of guilt and blame, allowing me to face reality and truth. Thank you for a way of escaping situations and relationships that were not right for me. You are ever faithful. I extol you from the depths of my heart with thanksgiving.

Cocoon

i want to come out of this cocoon that i'm in

is it time….
is it time?

i have been hiding so long
wrapped in the warmth of a quill that entangles my flesh
created to secure me
i have been hidden so long

i have vision

i can see my beauty

i am becoming a colorful butterfly set free to wander anywhere i want to go

i have no limits when i am free
my wings will elevate me
to higher heights

when i have grown

you will see

in time

in time

juanita parker

Thank you Lord for the seasons of quiet and non-activity. Thank you for renewal and development. I bless this space.

Destination

the things you go through in life
just to envision some sense of direction

the things you go through in life
just to attain a symbol of success

the things you go through in life
just to survive the stress and pressure

the things you go through in life
in order to focus and persevere on the path you have chosen

the things you go through in life
to prove yourself worthy of the goals you have set

the things you go through in life
just to make a degree of success, meaningful

after you have done all
been all
said all
after all the things you go through in life
while others rave, praise and applaud your accomplishments
still you will feel as if you have achieved nothing
if within the boundaries of walls you find yourself, alone and deserted
by the one you loved most, while on your journey.

juanita parker

Thank you Lord for the opportunity you have placed in my path to function in the capacity for which I am purposed. I press on eagerly looking forward to the next task without having any regret. Let your love flow through me and towards me. Let my disposition and character be filled with joy, peace, gentleness, goodness and faith. When I come to a place that feels empty, honor me with your presence, cover me with your warmth and love, so I may never feel lost and alone.

Elevate

have faith in God
move up a little higher

believe in yourself
move up a little higher

elevate your mind
move up a little higher

live your dreams
move up a little higher

energize your thinking
move up a little higher

eliminate all negative thoughts
move up a little higher

add some trust,
move up a little higher

vision is a step towards success
take the step, and
move up a little higher

Thank you for another chance to be complete in my heart, mind and spirit, to do your will and to follow the vision that you have given me. With this thought, I surrender.

Abandonment

once bathed in precious oils like a new born baby massaged with olive oil to keep its skin supple, soft and smooth, the reigns of my strength walked, swimmed and floated in the whirlpool of life sparked with the sensation of a burning fire that oozed out the fragrance of roses, violets and lilacs, like an aromatic perfume filtrating the air with irresistible warmth enticing me to reach to the center of my emotions to extend the source of my life's every beat of rhythm, burning in ecstasy, while strolling in seventh heaven;

like a thief in the night, along came a smoldering, bodacious, furious wind swirlin', twirlin', huffin' and puffin' like a tornado scoopin' and sprawlin' excavating precious land leaving scattered, shattered broken pieces, remnants of what used to be innocent, warm and free;

stooping to find the pieces to reconstruct, to mend what was once owned guiltless and naïve, sporting trust and belief that it was everlasting, only to find defeat and disbelief that it could happen to me; again, reaching into the center of my emotions to extend the source of my life's every beat of rhythm to rebuild and make it whole, only to discover the opened door was a hallow vacant land of devastation blocked by a wall –
somebody,
please, tell me,
what happened to my heart?
where did my heart go?

juanita parker

Dear Lord, sometimes the issues of my heart are many. I lay them before you and ask for healing and renewal. Please teach me where to place my values and how to protect the precious possession you gave to me, the life force of my heart. Keep me from the destruction that I may cause myself and others. You are my protector. Help me to make right decisions. Give me wisdom and discernment in all my endeavors. Thank you Lord for hearing me.

Been There – May Go Again

heartache and heartbreak
from some of the craziest circumstances
on the other hand, it wears away
because of resilience
and the ability to overcome
mysteriously we seem to find a way to bounce back

have you ever been so emotionally overwhelmed
to the degree that you could not speak
all you could do was sit and stare
into the atmosphere like a space cadet?

or have you ever felt so numb that you couldn't cry?
or found yourself searching for relief
searching for a word of confidence
from somebody
who could help you to regain
your composure and strength

devastating, devastating—

that's what infatuation will do
and you still go back
to try it again
is the joke on you?
listen, never pick apples on April Fool's day

juanita parker

Thank you Lord for the mistakes I have made that caused me heartache and pain, that strengthened my inner and outer person causing me to learn from my experiences. Thank you for growth. Now I understand more about wisdom.

Arrival

it is time to move to another plateau of
experience and reward
but for heaven's sake
forget about self-sacrifice
i finally learned
i am not a sacrificial lamb
i refuse to be a victim
i will enjoy freedom of expression
freedom of life
freedom to be who i am
where i am
no matter what you think
yes, i will
and if you can't deal with it
that's
your problem
because
i have arrived
with the determination
to be all I was created to be
I am not you
and you most definitely are not me

Thank you Lord for teaching me to put my trust in you. I seek you out to find my path and trails of assignments as I go through the mission fields of life.

Solitude

a place of quiet
a place of peace
a place where
I can retreat
in the mist of my home
with no one around
I light a candle to focus my mind
I close my eyes and inhale the scents
I breathe in and out
to feel the pulsation of my heart beat
and I breathe

solitude
a quiet place
sometimes the splash of waves
and grains of sand
flowing through my fingers
slowly descending
from my hand
I close my eyes and listen
to sounds
that engulf the air
on the cold ground
birds chirping
sea gulls flying
waves rushing to shore
no movement from me
my mind is in a trance

solitude
as I enter the door
I find my spirit there
I dream
I think
I meditate
I find pleasure

juanita parker

        in a world full of activity
        and stress
        there's contentment
        I can now rest
        thank God
        for solitude
        I can breathe
        freely in peace
        at last

Thank you Lord for places to retreat when my soul is weary and cries for recovery.

juanita parker

Image

The personification of something you can become

If you can understand it

If you can visualize it

If you can take on its attributes

If you are willing to walk in its spirit

If you are willing to let go of your will

If you are willing to let go of fear

If you are willing to believe it

Be prepared to receive your dreams

Come Soothe My Soul

Thank you Lord for teaching me how to let go, so I can be free to soar and get back on track accepting responsibility for my insufficiencies. Thank you for visions and dreams.

Pondering Thoughts

Trying times are opportunities that either make you a great success or a great disaster.

Sitting around feeling sorry for yourself only delays your future.

Faith is stepping out into the unknown until it becomes reality; then you start all over again with boldness.

Rejection can give you strength to conquer the impossible.

Trusting in people can lead you to a dead-end, but dead-ends will lead you to God.

When you discover that God is totally the source, then you will soar like an eagle.

Originality is creating something from nothing that initiates from within.

Time and energy are the fuels that ignite creativity.

It is the unknown that frightens me.

Face fear head on. Analyze fear; find out what is real and what is not.

Use fear as a motivating force and take action.

Expectation of failure is thinking about all the bad things that can possibly happen that will probably never happen.

Prepare for the task ahead.

There's no need to compare yourself with others for you too are an individual with unique talents and untapped potential; all you need to do is find it.

Discuss and utilize your own uniqueness.

The greatest competition is competing with yourself.

Learning from failure is a step-ladder to success.

Listening to your inner voice helps you find inner strength.

juanita parker

Thank you Lord for the lessons we learn from our experiences and from others. As you nourish my mind, heart and actions allow me to walk with a renewed spirit of empowerment, remembering the lessons I've learned on the path of my journey.

Ode To My Friend, Terri

        bangles and beads,
        mountains and trees,
        money and men
        children and kin
        heartache and pain
        loss and gain
        fun and games
        say it again
        still we are friends

The first time I met her, it was not as if we were strangers. Our husbands were best friends and I was the newcomer. And of course, since we would probably see a lot of each other, due to that fact, the socially correct thing to do was to make a formal introduction over dinner.

It was the last part of summer right before dusk, when I arrived at her home for dinner. We talked and shared our ideas about the material things we liked.

Immediately, she beckoned me to stroll towards her bedroom, where we girl-talked sharing our likes, dislikes and favorite subjects – fashionable clothes – designer's of course—fashionable cars – only the sporty high-ticketed ones – entertainment and money.

Her new bedroom suite had just arrived and as we talked, she went to her closet and pulled out material and a formal dress pattern she was getting tailor-made in black lace and silk satin.

She even pulled from her closet a short mink skirt designed for dual purposes. It was a jacket and skirt that she wore one of three ways, attached as a coat, separate as a skirt or a mink jacket –if you please—made from the remnants of a full mink coat she no longer wanted to wear—as a full-length mink, that is. I thought it was a brilliant design. I would never have worn it, but for her, that was just fine.

Only weeks had passed after our social event that we exchanged cars just for fun. Hers was a pink hardtop Grandprix, while mine was a silver-gray convertible Mustang—both cars were new, of course.

juanita parker

Together, we were two bubbly-young socialites full of enthusiasm, excited about our dreams and life. Our futures looked promising. To this day;

>We've had our ups;
>We've had our downs;
>We've had our losses;
>We've had our gains;
>But most of all,
>We remain the best
>as lifetime friends.

Come Soothe My Soul

Thank you Lord for sending friends to walk with, talk with, laugh with, pray with, and sometimes cry with. Friends who enjoy just being together no matter what the circumstances.

juanita parker

Ode To My Hair

When I was a little girl,
Mamma always put a part in the middle of my head and created two braids on the top of my head like a tiara, as if I was somebody's princess –
If I was so royal, why didn't I like wearing my crisscrossed braided crown, everyday?

I wanted to wear my hair loose like other little girls.
In a pony tail, in curls,
But Mamma said –
I was different,
my hair was thick, and I was too tender-headed to even think about it.—
As a matter of fact, she just didn't feel like hurting me while combing and pulling my hair so hard 'til I cried.

When I became an adult,
I cut my hair,
I let it grow,
I wear curls,
I wear my hair loose,
I wear my hair nappy,
I wear my hair braided, and not everybody
can do that!

Yes, Mamma was right.
I am different,
That makes me feel real special—
Just like a princess.

Come Soothe My Soul

Thank you Lord for every strand of hair on my head.
Thank you for nourishing it with health and strength.
Thank you for making it the crown you placed on my head to distinguish me from all the others.

juanita parker

Ode To The DJ

Oh, I'm so glad to hear you again.
It's been so long.
I often think about the first time we met,
I was entranced by your music and words.
You're so gifted; you're so strong,
Please enchant me with your charms,
and do something for me,

please?

Play me a love song.
I've waited for this moment so long.
You know how to express
when I can't do my best
in saying I'm happy or blue.

Bring on the harmony.
Let my soul feel the melody
Please,
Play me a love song
yes,
that's the one—
Now I can dance the night away.

Come Soothe My Soul

Thank you Lord for music. Thank you for a variety I can choose from. Thank you for the joy and comfort it brings. Thank you for allowing me to hear it, sing it, and play it. Thank you for allowing me to move freely and swiftly expressing my soul.

juanita parker

Power In The Name Of Jesus

I was feeling overwhelmed
about the circumstances in my life
all bills were due
my refrigerator was empty
I needed an automobile too

I searched for an answer

An angel of the Lord whispered in my ear
encouraging words saying

Praise and pray, praise and pray
there's power in the name of Jesus
don't fall out, don't faint in vain
an answer is on the way

You never know from which door
God will meet your needs
He uses faithful servants
who go where the Spirit leads

How quickly we forget
when our lives are in a mess
the power we have been given
to praise and pray with thanksgiving
God is faithful in every way…

even in putting food on the table

Thank you Lord for meeting my needs. Your provisions are always perfect. Thank you for rescuing me always in the nick of time.

juanita parker

Revival

I. The Situation

I was down in the depths of the valley.
I could not speak;
I could not sing;
I could not praise;
I could not cry;
I could not worship.

My soul cried out and my flesh was weak

What has come over me, where is the joy of my salvation?
Where are you Holy Spirit?

II. Stillness

Is this a time to be still?
Is this a time to listen?
Is this a time to change?
Is this a time for renewal?

I am lost.
All I can do is wait.
I am like a woman
bound in mummy cloth.
[Silence]

III. Requests

Rejuvenate my spirit,
Rejuvenate my soul,
Remove this toxic glitch
that's trying to tear me apart.

Am I angry?
Yes, I am angry.
Am I hurt?
Yes, I am hurt.

Do I want to cry?
Yes, I want to cry.

I feel so numb.

Revive my spirit; give me direction.
My soul is thirsty.
Please, fill me with your living water.

IV. Inquiry

What is it that you want of me Lord?
Help me to understand.

You have planted me;
You have rooted me;
I am not a wandering child;

I love you;
I adore you;
I praise you.

juanita parker

V. Assurance

You are good to me;
I know that you love me.
I know you are with me—
Even, when I cannot feel your presence.

VI. Testimony

I cried furiously, loudly
So God would hear my prayers.

Thereafter I searched for His Spirit.
I went to the house of the Lord.
I was not in my own city,
when I heard a familiar Word.

I returned home, and was led
to a different place to worship.
I was restless
but I soon relaxed,
seeking out His Word.

I listened so intensely;
I refused to let go of Him.
I searched for God because my soul was thirsty;
I needed guidance and direction;
A spiritual blessing from Him.

VII. Answer

It was early one Sunday morning when the words of the preacher swooped the air like a sharpened arrow directed to pierce my soul while sermonizing in the flow of a cadence:

Now is the time, now is the time.
Get out your creativity.
You have too much creativity to let it go to waste.
Get out all of those writings,
visions and dreams that you have stored away.
Get out all of those goals that you have written down. Write, create music, sing,
Now is the time.

The instructions were direct and specific;
perfectly timed for me
The preached Word met my needs;
Suddenly, I became free
from the turmoil in my spirit;
I felt so relieved.

I went to the alter to pray,
an intercessor met me there
as we stood and agreed
I felt His presence in the center;
I thanked God for relief

VIII. Rejoice

I left the House of the Lord.
The power of His Spirit was extremely strong upon me.
It flowed within me like the rapids of a waterfall.
It was so refreshing,
in the depths of my belly
I groaned.

VX. Revived

When I returned home, and opened my front door
I quickly fled to an empty space.
I laid face down before the Lord, a spring of living water flooded the depths of my inner spirit while I audibly spoke words of thanksgiving and praise.
I went on and on for hours;
My soul was refreshingly quenched;
I laughed and cried in the presence of the Lord;
From the depths of the valley
my soul was revived.

Come Soothe My Soul

Thank you Lord for recovery, spiritually, mentally, emotionally and physically. Thank you for letting me survive the traumas of my own desires and mistakes. Thank you for leading me to higher ground.

juanita parker

Direction

As I continue on a spiritual path,
I am a servant with a dream.
I trust that someone will be encouraged
to follow where God leads.

Come Soothe My Soul

Thank you Lord for leading my feet in the paths that you have blazed for me. Thank you for allowing me to meet strangers on the way who desire in their hearts to know the way to salvation.

juanita parker

Tool For The Mission

God specifically created a unique person
When he created you
Just like he specifically gave you purpose
And some work to do
With a little patience, hope
Love and faith
Mixed with wisdom, knowledge and persistence
You're the tool totally equipped
To complete the mission

Thank you Lord for all the tools you have created to fortify my person with strength to do as you have directed me to do.

juanita parker

Alter Call

It was Sunday morning
the choir was singing down to the bone
the shouts were loud,
the cries were moans
the preacher got up
now that's a fact you know
everybody was quiet
nobody walked out the door

bless you sister, bless you brother
was his opening remarks
in a deep and mellow authoritative voice

when he got down to business
and took his text
he looked up and said,
today, I invite you to
come with me to John 3:16

he waited a moment
and began to read
"For God so loved the world,
that he gave his only begotten Son,
that whosoever believeth in him should not perish,
but have everlasting life."

My subject today is
"Believe and You Shall Be Saved"

With a solemn voice he began to speak
he delivered the message
everybody was on their feet

when he was finished
he extended his hand
the altar was ready
for lost souls in demand

Come Soothe My Soul

While he stood beckoning
the choir began to sing
a song with words that
supported the message

The clock on the wall is ticking
it's time to pray my brother
it's time to pray for
the sin sick soul

The clock on the wall is ticking
and it won't be long
Jesus is coming back again

Open your heart my sister
Jesus is the way
open your heart my brother
receive him today
He'll forgive you of your sins
surrender your life to Him

to be saved, Jesus is the only way.

It was Sunday afternoon
and many came and prayed
to accept Jesus as their Lord and Savior
with abundant life to hold
fulfillment was in their souls
an answer gained
a promise made
salvation was found at the alter

juanita parker

Thank you Lord for the love you have for me and for giving your life to cover my sins. Thank you for the richest gift ever to be given.

Seasons

I know that there is a season and purpose for everything
I believe it; I see it.

There are times when I have to recollect myself;
Release the bondage to bring back my freedom,
It is difficult when everybody has a piece of me, but me –
Flesh and things dictating my life,
Extracting my existence from reality.

Where have I been all of these years?
What have I done with myself?
Did I give too much of myself away?
Have I forfeited my mission?

So now, here we are, mind, soul and spirit
Wrapped in one body waiting for God.
Then God emerges–as only God can
Speaking to my soul, telling me
It is time for change.
The finale to this episode is over.
Move on,
I have plans for you.

For a moment I could not move; I was afraid;
I was fearful; I was distraught; I was angry.
Change is hard to deal with.
But there comes a time for every purpose
And God must deal with me.
I must follow his directions;
I must follow his lead, for me.
No other can fill my unique shoes
When God calls, it is my time to be all I can be –
Even with my bag of issues,
Even with my hurts, aches and pains,
I will go where I'm led – to fulfill my purpose, for the season.

juanita parker

Dear Lord, I may not do everything in the time that the eyesight of man perceive, but your perfect timing is all that is needed. Thank you for your promises and giving me patience to wait on you.

Trials and Tribulations

Trials and tribulations grow us.
Trials and tribulations force us to rise above defeat.
The intensity within our being clings willingly onto strength,
assisting us to rise above the obstacles,
no matter what the current says.

When trials and tribulations approach us,
our ears are open wide,
listening for the roaring wind
that comes to be our guide.
How we listen and follow
depends upon an urgent need
to progress in our endeavors,
eagerly waiting to succeed.

While going through the flames of the process,
striving to fulfill our dreams,
Trials and tribulations
produces progress,
a part of how
successes are achieved.

juanita parker

Thank you Lord for the trials and tribulations that have influenced my character making me stronger.

The Quest Of Love

Love goes beyond emotions and passion
Love tears down walls of stone
Love's influence conquers hatred
Love,
Love's character is filled with peace

Love understands the mysteries of the heart
Love seeks out happiness for the disgruntled
Love's persona makes one warm and content
Love's very nature enhances trust that binds
Love yearns to heal the wounds of time

Love strives to forgive and to forget
Love's temperament retains no grudges
Love is free in giving, seeking nothing in return
Love's strength is compassionate and tender

Love is benevolent in season and out
Love is caring, patient and loyal
Love is the source of a predestined plan
Love is perceptive and wise

Love is discerning, thoughtful in mind
Love is observant, gentle and kind
Love is considerate towards another's need
Love is gracious in service and hospitable deeds

Love goes beyond the exterior, and seeks the spirit within
Love appreciates beauty beneath the skin
Love's power is strength in times of weakness
Love,
Love promotes generosity

Love esteems itself beyond the heights of fear
Love supercedes obsession within emotions
Love knows the difference between it and infatuation
Love is committed and submissive

juanita parker

Love,
Love is the transaction of two becoming one—
Love is the inspiration to greatness
Love is victorious and valued in life

Love is filled with jubilation
Love's fragrance increases with adoration
Love's heart encourages devotion
Love binds the tides of time with faith and hope

Love is the example set by God the Father and His Son
Love reigns above all things;
And above all,
God is love.

Thank you Lord for the capacity to love. Please keep my passion pure in heart, mind and spirit, so I can be an effective servant.

juanita parker

Jubilance

Like an angel gliding smoothly from heaven,
you adorned my opened window in the still of night;
I was simply praying,
you listened to every word,
healed my spirit,
mended my soul,
giving me the opportunity to rise
above my circumstances,
obstacles and destruction.

It is the stability of your everlasting love
and the connection with your power,
that continuously fortifies my life
as I go from mountain top to mountain top
leaping higher and higher,
dancing and singing,
shouting and praising.
You answered my prayer;
by giving me jubilant joy.

Thank you Lord for encouragement, new direction, guidance and another chance.

juanita parker

The Power Of Fear

Fear will devastate you
and cause you to retreat
from everything that is progressive
in your life's feat
but you can overcome it
with boldness along the trail
control it with force
and clear the air;

Analyze the cause of fear
stare it right in the face
soon you will discover
fear's motive
is working hard
to knock you
out of the race;

Think of fear as an inflated balloon
the more air you blow into it
the larger it will become
deflate the rubber thing
and it will not exist
flimsy of its fuel
it has no real strength;

So, empty your mind
don't give fear any favor
become completely aware
that fear is an impostor
positioned to postpone your dreams
but only if you let it –

Stand firm, don't waiver
no matter what the test
know all things are possible
when you believe in your vision,
believe in your dreams,
believe you can achieve them –
All Things…

Come Soothe My Soul

Dear Lord deliver me from fear of the unknown, fear of what I don't know that causes me upheaval, confusion and distrust. Please secure me with unwavering faith. Thank you for helping me to overcome fear.

juanita parker

Transition

It's easy to allow your eyes to visualize your obsessions forcing sirens of your imagination to take you on a roller coaster ride while feeling sorry for yourself especially when you look in the mirror and convince yourself that

you're getting older

you're too fat

there's a permanent frown line in your face,

you're not as attractive as you used to be—

Well, while moving from one phase to another

here's a positive point of view

if you can pinch yourself

and say ouch!

that's a miracle

be happy, there's so much more you can do

because you still have life

Thank you Lord for life, I am grateful that you still use me to sow seeds, to water the ground and to reap the benefits of my labors.

juanita parker

Creativity

I shall never forget the time
I shared the thoughts on my mind,
It was in a song
But you refused to listen

I gave you harmony
I gave you melody
I gave you prose
But you were never satisfied with my views—
my thoughts—the expressions of my heart
Yet, you kept on harassing me

You took me through tribulations, agony and pain
You pulled at my emotions
laughed at my tears—
And trampled on my insecurities

Sometimes you treated me as if you loved me
Then you turned around and took away the flow
Leaving me to suffer
void of understanding
void of vigor
void of passion
I was weightless under your mysterious spell
And you thought
your sting had conquered, me?

Oh! No!—I am in control

I'm going to conquer you like David conquered Goliath—
Like Delilah conquered Samson—
Like the fire of the dragon—
You have become my burning source—
I am purified through your flame
intrigued by your mystique

Come Soothe My Soul

You have enchanted me
You will hear me when I call
You will listen when I speak
You will assist me with all my endeavors
As I sit down to produce
to design
to introduce the words that are on my mind
compose a melody
recite a poem
I demand your undivided attention

Creativity
in the palm of my hand,
in the midst of my heart
through the mirror in my mind
you will not escape, but
you will serve, me.

juanita parker

Thank you Lord for making me in your image and giving me the gift of creativity, imagination, foresight and the ability and freedom to express it.

Inspiration

my inspiration comes from love
love motivated from heaven above
love that invigorates
allowing my soul to escape
to a higher terrain

my inspiration is strong
it carries me through turbulent storms
myriad of thoughts
embrace me with peace
while tides rush in
to soothe my feet

my inspiration is prayer
for God is always there
I talk to Him, He talks to me
He guides me everywhere

my inspiration is God's Word
it strengthens my life's design
I meditate,
He invigorates
my mind to understand
that all that is
and all that shall be
does not exist
without Him;
my inspiration comes from God

juanita parker

Thank you Lord for the way you inspire my thoughts and ignite my mind with a burning desire to achieve what I seek after.

Melodic Motion

lost in the episodes of sound
when the music plays

jugglin' my thoughts to comprehend
the memories it brings

splashes of rhythm sweep through my soul

binding me
piercing me
making me whole

lasting memories flood my mind
steering me towards episodes in time

streams of joy
sometimes emotional sadness

I can't get away

when the music plays

juanita parker

Thank you Lord for ears to hear the melodic sounds of instruments and voice. Majestically uniting together in harmonies, patterns and movements that satisfy my inner soul stirring the pulse of my heartbeat. Soothing, calming, beautiful music.

Light

i was innocent

i was vulnerable

i was covered in darkness under the shadow of a veil

my thoughts were mingled with one point of view

i must follow the path

i don't know where I'm going

but I'll know when I'm there

for light will appear

juanita parker

Thank you Lord for helping me to see things from different perspectives not just from my own point of view, allowing me to explore truths and opportunities that knock at the door of my mind.

Enslaved

while traveling through time
there are many issues that plague
my mind
to be
to fly like eagles soar
to have joy
peace
to be free
to reminisce
over the good times
the bad
to laugh
to cry
to be happy
to be sad

for me
to possess strength
yet suffer
in the hands of
hatred, shame
murder, abuse
heartache, excruciating pain
for society's sake
for history's sake
like the children of Israel
but not like the children of Israel
still
not by my will
with all I've been through
all I've been forced to do

I can never forget
when I try to reminisce
the thoughts are not there
of foliage land
of mineral mines
of gold

juanita parker

of ancestors
generations ago
stolen, divided
conquered, deprived
defrauded, enslaved
deceived
I pray
I cry
justice
will abide
my soul will never rest in peace
'til my children have
liberty
reparation
dignity
for sweat
for tears
for injustice
for division
for pain
more than two hundred years
in a land
of liberty and
justice for all
a home
called brave
brave, but
still
not
free

Dear Lord, I intercede on behalf of all people who have been and still are enslaved, abused and mistreated by other human beings all over the world. I pray for deliverance of children who suffer from the hands of wickedness, whose innocence has been tampered with, demeaned and snuffed out. Please have mercy upon us and forgive our trespasses as we forgive.

Energy

Energy, the flow of a surrounding force producing a stream of vitality you cannot visibly see, for it is known only by the surrender of a productive, electrifying, zestful spirit moving swiftly to usurp the electric power it brings.

When you began to discover that you are not self-made or self-existing, the connection becomes clear, especially when you think of energy in the atmosphere. You are a mechanism running on the stream and force of something greater than you. The Creator of life is the power source of energy igniting you.

As a universal magnet, the synthesis of propelled motion is compiled of contagious kinetic energy. When you take of its substance and retreat to collect your breath, kinetic energy still never runs out, it just keeps on flowing with activity and life, bouncing back and forth, back and forth in the universe.

But at some point energy takes on another purpose when the human flesh takes its rest, leaving only the spirit to take energy quickly into flight, as it vanishes in the air, bringing it to brand new life, soaring back into heaven.

Thank you Lord for invigorating my mind, body and soul with energy so I can do the things that I have been assigned. I do not take it for granted. I am grateful. Please give me the wisdom to keep my physical body in tune through good health practices and exercise. Give me the wisdom to prepare and eat healthy foods that will help me to stay physically in shape.

I rid myself of toxic foods, drinks and drugs that are destructive and unhealthy for my body's sake. I now replace them with nurturing food and water to keep my body, mind and soul purified.

juanita parker

Bravery

Yes, fear bears the ambiance of dread
and unwarranted concern,
anxiety and worry that does the body harm.

Yes, fear creates phobias in the mind
and causes untruths to exist,
but if you are motivated
and possess a burning desire
to complete your tasks,
even fear will bow down to bravery.

Dear Lord, when I recognize fear, help me to use it as a stepping stone and not a hindrance. Allow me to overcome my fears in all circumstances so I can accomplish and finish what I set out to do.

juanita parker

Panic Attack

One summer evening, a friend and I got in the car, put on a taped sermon and drove south towards the Pacific Ocean. By our instincts, we drove into the hills trying to locate a place where we could view beautiful mansions and the ocean at the same time, but it turned extremely dark, as I recall.

While listening to the sermon, entitled "When You've Come to a Dead-end Road," – the circumstances we found ourselves in was exactly, that! – We had come to a dark, dead-end road.

In my ears, the preacher's eloquent vocal expression began to stand out like an emergency alert, as he cadenced, "don't cry, don't panic because you can't hear," while my inner voice stood up silently screaming like a little spoiled brat, "how about, because we can't see!" At the time, we were quite a distance into the mountains with the high-beam car lights on, – still the velvet darkness only allowed us to see a few feet in front of us. There were no houses, just hills, a narrow road and us.

I could feel my friend's tension as she began to get a little insecure and frightened. And of course, me and my bravery softly responded to her character and said, "don't be afraid, just follow the path." Yet, even that moment presented my stomach with a few butterflies, but afterwards, it was only a matter of seconds before joy swept over us as we entered on the three-laned highway that displayed lights and a definite path.

That particular circumstance of the evening penned my mind with an indelible ink transcribing words, telling me that there are some uncertainties that will cause us to panic as we venture through the path of life. Even with a charted course, in some instances the path will still present detours and uncertainties surrounded by unexpected circumstances. But through faith, patience and trust, if we are persistent, determined and willing to follow the road to the dead-end, soon we will discover a luminous light and helping hand to lead us safely to our destination, giving us the opportunity to explore more new adventures. There is light after darkness—Don't Panic!

Come Soothe My Soul

Dear Lord, keep me on course towards my destination. If I must be detoured point me in the direction that I should go allowing me the opportunity to quickly get back on the road.

juanita parker

Three Requests

Three mature women had one request each when they came to visit me. One wanted a cassette tape of music, the other a bottle of 273 perfume; and the third wanted a jar of cashews. I just happened to have had those items right on hand. I experienced amazing joy in fulfilling their wishes.

It is wonderful to honor people who have reared and nourished us to the point of adulthood. They stand with us in our life decisions and deserve honor and respect for their dignity and commitment to us.

Through my exhilaration, a thought came into my mind. How much more joy does God have in giving to me my request when I honor him with respect and obedience in the things he request of me.

For everyone who asks receives; he who seeks finds; and to him who knocks, the door will be opened. Matthew 7:8

Dear Lord, thank you for provisions and allowing me to give to others. Thank you for relatives.

Supportive People

It is so wonderful to have someone
who says I believe in you.
Someone who share your works and dreams
just being supportive

On any given day
when you need a helping hand
they show up to assist you
with a smile on their face
they are positive
they encourage you
with a warm word or deed
they are very seldom idle
in what they undertake
they seem to have some magic
that puts a smile on your face

They are special loving people
who enjoy the things you do
who know how to receive a gift
while they give of themselves to you

They take the time to listen
to all that's on your mind
they even take you with them
in their heart, thoughts and prayers
special loving people
supportive in all their ways
they make other people happy
sharing themselves in very unselfish ways

Lord thank you for people that you send my way to help and assist me with the work I have been called to do. Thank you for their love, patience and support. Bless them in every way, let their hopes and dreams be fulfilled.

juanita parker

Valuable Woman

I am a valuable woman treading through the process of life. I am a contributor towards humanity's well-being. I have many talents, gifts and dreams. I communicate with other valuable women. I esteem my sisters as we communicate to make our universe a better place to live in. We view life with truth and reality realizing we have opportunities to progress together as we proceed to genuinely be supportive of one another.

When I think about my world, the questions I ask are how and what can I contribute to make it a better place. I have a place in our society and in order for me to contribute to it, I aspire to broaden my scope and perspectives towards people.

I welcome opportunities to create a network embracing diverse relationships along with my sisters. We learn from each other. We not only replenish the earth but we also water it with love and respect. As we grow, we connect and graft others into the mechanism of life, learning from our mistakes and growing to higher levels so our children and children's children will reap great rewards from the fruit of our labor.

Come Soothe My Soul

Dear Lord thank you for sisters I have come to know, and for those whom I have come in contact with recently and those I have yet to meet. They are my extended family. Together create in us the desire to move beyond envy, jealousy, superficial ways and attitudes. Thank you for what we have learned from each other and the growth from our experiences and challenges. Thank you for mentoring, love and understanding.

Communing With God

Lord, I trust in you. I wait on you and the power of your anointing. You open doors. You make my life worthwhile. You alone are perfect in all your ways. It is to your power and glory that I worship and give you praise. It is to your honor that I bow in submission to your will.

I now move forward in the arena designated for me. I have resolved to use the tools that you have given me with vigor, persistence, understanding and wisdom desiring to continuously learn what I need to learn in order to do the work effectively. I know that you never break a promise and all things will come to pass as you have said. I persist to be an obedient servant. Thank you for helping me.

Diligence

My eyes are wide open;
The spotlight is angled on you.
Encumbered by the affairs of life
I watch you stumble and fall;
Yet even then,
You have enduring strength
To grow.

Your focus is centered;
Your sight is full of vision and dreams.
You have refused to let anything
Dismantle your soaring wings.

From start to finish, you persist,
Even when it's inconvenient.
The character you possess
Makes you a precious stone
Priceless, you will become.

As the jagged edges are being chiseled away
You will be presented the most desirable jewel;
Smooth, sparkling, brilliant, bright and shiny,
The artistic work of a master craftsman;

You are worth more than anything
Money can buy, whether silver or gold,
All because your coat of armor
Is engraved with
Diligence.

juanita parker

Dear Lord thank you for your delicate touch and understanding as I grow into the person you want me to be. Thank you for your tender mercy and protection.

Trust

I have felt your pain,
won't you let go of it
I can handle it better than you

I've seen your tears
felt your fears
and the hurt within your heart
I know what you've been through
from all the horrific choices

I have seen you sit on grains of sand
gazing over the ocean
trying to find peace of mind
and solutions to your problems
at last you've found the open door
to the problem solver

Trust me, for I am the way
to make you whole and complete
dwell in my presence
walk in faith
not by sight
I have mercy and abundant life

your destined future is no secret to me
if you will follow my lead,
surrender, rest,
put your trust in me and
I will take you there

juanita parker

Thank you Lord for being my overseer and protector. Thank you for knowing all about me. Thank you for nudging me and directing me towards righteousness and guiding me where I should go.

Today

Today, situations around me are stressful—work, people acting unusual causing me distress at the most inopportune time in my life—and the storm continues.— Even so, I believe in my dreams; rest assured I will see them through, for they shall be.

Oh God, how difficult it is to let go of those things I love, those things that I do so well and feel comfortable with. You have taught me faith, now once again, please help me to exercise my faith and trust in you. I don't intentionally doubt and fear; it's just the unknown that frightens me because I have yet to experience what I cannot see.

Oh God, you have been faithful to me in the past, over the small steps and the large. These steps I now take are not unfamiliar but the path is new. I want to go where you are leading me. My spirit is eager to follow you. In the depths of my being, I feel the very presence of your Spirit leading me.

Oh God, help me to exercise my faith and trust in you. I cannot depend on man; he has let me down so many times. I only have you to see me through.

Oh God, please help me to completely trust and depend on you.

Bless the Lord oh my soul and forget not his benefits. Ps. 103:2

juanita parker

Thank you Lord for always being faithful to me. Thank you for rescuing me when I am at my weakest point. I come to you in prayer. I seek you out like a child seeking after her parents for comfort and guidance. As my Father, you are always there to hear me. It is your goodness and mercy that follows me guiding my every step. I am so grateful that I can always come to you.

Instant Replay

He said, "You're drawing me,"
I said, "No I'm not"
He said, "Yes you are"
I said, "No I'm not"
He said, "Yes you are" and swiftly
opened his arms wide, bent over and embraced me.
My heart felt the warmth of his tender touch while the rafters of my soul jumped up and down as if the wings of a giant angel were compassionately hugging me.
He would not let me go, so I looked into his eyes and said,
"Can we do that scene one more time – You're drawing me!"

juanita parker

Dear Lord: Sometimes your spirit draws me when I am weak, sometimes your spirit draws me when I am strong. Even though I don't see you face to face with human eyes, I can feel your presence surrounding me through the Holy Spirit burning in the depths of my soul. The yearning in my heart to be in your presence returns me to your throne over and over. Thank you for your magnetic power.

The Miracle Of Voice Tones

when you talk to me
I want to hear a pleasant tone
the miracle of its reflection
will give you a sweet response

vulgarity and name-calling
is so profane and not my point of view
I exist with integrity
my lifestyle is not demeaning

abusive words causes mental anguish
and some times physical harm
and that is just not for me
I was not created a punching bag
but a loving delightful person
you see,

a kind word will make all the difference
in the type of response you receive
from me or anyone
then together we can experience
love, happiness, peace and
a delightful atmosphere
within the miracle of a loving voice tone.

juanita parker

Dear Lord, make me mindful of my tone of voice. Help me to use it in a loving manner. Remove edginess and any offensive attitude or anger. Teach me how to speak with kind and thoughtful words. Let me not cause anyone harm or deliver strife with my tongue.

Tina Allen, You Are Distinctively...

Talented with dexterity, mastery and skill
God sent you to make a difference
in the lives of people around the world
as you give of yourself
through the inventions of your hands.

You are inspiring to those you encounter
with wisdom from the heart,
articulate in deliberation,
imparting knowledge, foresight and thought;

Nourished with vision,
focused from above,
endowed with a gift,
because of God's love.

Anointed to construct
as The Lord commanded you,
sculpturing the legacy of trailblazers,
leaving a path for youth.

Tina, Tina—the Angels whisper,
your name shall be written
on the golden plate of history
for carving out legacies,
for holding on to truth,
for freeing worthy spirits,
from the web of time,
for this very purpose,
you are distinctively God's perfect design.

juanita parker

Thank you Lord for talented and gifted people who have burning flames of fire within their souls to use their talents and gifts to bring people and nations together for the good of the total human race. Blessed are the peacemakers for they shall see God.

The Creed Of A Wise Woman

like an eagle flies,
prepared to rise above the storms of life
so does a wise woman—

loving God first, then herself
gives her the strength she needs
with confidence she
passes love on
to those who are much in need

her conversation is uplifting
inspiring, pleasant and firm
she speaks encouraging words of praise
to teach little boys and girls

she possesses good understanding,
wisdom and knowledge
walks worthy in her path
she is benevolent in spirit
a joyful soul
prepared to meet the tasks

she is mentally intelligent
articulate when she speaks
sometimes she's very funny
she will even kiss your cheek

she is full of goodness and mercy
with gracious finesse
to win the heart of a king
she is blessed and favored
she knows what honor means

she is a consistent warrior
she knows how to start a day
she has a secret closet
where she retreats to pray

juanita parker

she is a precious jewel
whom God has dressed with grace
she is covered with bravery and courage
as she travels from place to place

she is mindful of her mission
she has assignments every day
because she is a believer
she lets nothing disparage her way

in God she has placed her trust
her faith in Him is solid
there is no wavering in her thoughts
she is confident in her actions

she is a wise and competent finisher
in every thing she does
her deeds will remain a legacy
from earth to heaven above

Dear Lord, thank you for the many women who love you and strive to live by your principals.
Thank you for the work of their hands and loving deeds.
Thank you for their intellect, work and humanitarian acts.
Thank you for their sympathetic hearts towards the needs of our nation and world collectively.
Thank you for those who have stood in the gap and have taken risk to make the world a better place for women to progress.
Thank you for their nurturing and the ability to follow and lead.
Thank you for pouring out your spirit upon women.

juanita parker

Nurturing

It is not always easy to rise above adversity
when your mind
is filled with pollution
negative issues and conditions
that life and time has promoted

But when the mind is clear
and the heart is free
freedom lends a helping hand
to healthy nurturing

Jealousy is toxic
envy is so insane
we have so much in common
so why do we have to play games

Sister-girl and brother
life is just too short
to spend it with resentment
when together we can do so much

For centuries the enemy has attempted
to tear the family down
trying to divide and conquer
whom ever plays on his ground

Come Soothe My Soul

Trust is a key
to living in harmony and peace
to build a constructive future
with promise and not deceit

Learning to live together
reaching often to prayer
renewing our minds for progress
as we climb golden stairs
new horizons await us
as we take hold of the staff

With love towards one another
we will have strength in our numbers
moving to higher ground
building in everyway
because we have been rewarded
with a brand new day

juanita parker

Dear Lord, Thank you for giving us the desire to seek your face and to know you. Thank you for teaching us spiritual principles creating in us integrity and self-respect. Thank you for another chance.

Today, I Think I Met Him

i was walking in the flower mart
when he caught my eye
while picking up a potted orchid
he smoothly said, "how's it going?"
directly—to me!

the pallet in my throat
began to hinder my speech
while I spilled out stammering words,
i think,
i think, i'm okay!

my eyes glistened
as my ears opened wide
listening to the sound of melodic arpeggios

a symphony orchestra
an angelic choir
singing in the air

all at the same time
i glanced directly into his face
glimmering eyes
silky-smooth brown skin
beautiful white teeth
smiling in my face

no ring on his fingers
no diamonds in his ears
could this really be a single man
or a mirage
flirting with me

we struck up a conversation
about orchid cultivation
and the choices he had made
he said the diversity of orchids are delicate
somewhat like a woman,

juanita parker

you've got to treat them
with tender loving care
if you want them to be there

we stood talking for a moment
and started moving our feet
strolling to the coffee bar
where we immediately took a seat
he ordered a cappuccino
and said have what you please
I replied, thank you, I'll have a cup of tea

we were so engrossed in our conversation
we forgot that we didn't formally meet
his hello was filled with laughter
as he swiftly took my hand
when I looked into his eyes
I saw this beautiful inner man

he was thought provoking and articulate
with an interesting point of view
a heart of ideal compassion
keen intellect too

I was trying hard to contain myself
while presenting some mystique
he asked me out to dinner
and as I began to say, yes
a blazing siren invaded the air
my heart pulsated at every beck and beat
my head was in a daze
when I finally figured it out
the darn alarm clock was ringing
insisting it was time
for me to wake up!

Thank you Lord for an imagination that invigorates my thoughts towards my dreams. I look forward with hope towards sharing life with someone special to perfect my love, but first of all the most perfect love that I have, is you.

Experience

... we glory in tribulations also: knowing that tribulation worketh patience; and patience, experience; and experience hope...Romans 5:3

One glorious spring morning, I was on the cool sands of my favorite beach spending some quiet time seeking direction and answers for the struggles that I was going through.

I was deep in thought while glancing over the amazing Pacific Ocean's grandiosity that produced sprays of vapor that furiously rushed to shore to whisk me away into the raging tides, while the spirit of my soul worked hard to seek me out, to find, me.

I was grateful for the open space, grainy sand, creative artistry and splendid work of God as I absorbed the colorful reflections of a sky blue pallet producing white tides from the ocean's waves.

I believe in Jesus Christ; I am blessed to have him in my life. For every alarming trial, I have been assured of one thing, while calling on his name an answer to my struggle would surely come and the situation would soon cease. I know without him, I would not have made it to the point of deliverance or recovery for I have always needed added strength.

As I sat on the sand, I began to take inventory of the experiences in my life that helped to develop and reinforce my stability. Of course, I know I am not alone when I say; I still have so much more yet to learn. For one reason or another, like me, many have gone through something that has caused them to call on a higher authority. It is somewhat hilarious, yet serious, how we take ourselves through so much drama trying to prove ourselves to something, or somebody.

We compete for position; we compete for love trying to be impressive because we want to be accepted, even then we are still misunderstood.

We experience heartache and pain due to our own actions, yes, and other people's actions too that affect our emotions, mental attitude and survival, even our style of life. We stumble, fall, get up and return to the race of life with our baggage and issues in our hands, in search of recovery, ready and prepared to start all over again.

We have an insatiable desire to be wanted, needed and loved like the rest of the crowd. We get confused about doing things the right way as opposed to the wrong, and anything beyond that is due to a naïve mentality to some degree, mixed with untamed emotions which leads to experience that causes us to grow, a little wiser.

For me, life has not been an easy road. The lessons have been difficult to learn while making the same mistakes over and over. But one day, I got it.

You see the process of experience is not something that happens instantaneously, it develops in small proportions like walking up a staircase step by step. And whether good or not so good, there is always something to be pulverized and sifted, taught and learned.

Have you ever heard your inner voice saying no to you over something you wanted to do, that you should not have done but you did it anyway, only to find out that the outcome was not quite what you desired or expected? Then guilt stepped in echoing reprimands in your mind and ears speaking loud and clear – oh, if you had only listened the first time—but your stubbornness just would not let you? How often do we go through scenario after scenario indulging in instant replays while striving to push ourselves to get it together.

There were times when I created so much ridiculous chaos for myself that I questioned my own sanity. My fleshy appetite just would not allow me to keep myself away from the source that was inviting me to experience self-sabotage.

We sometimes clutch onto things and people for self-gratification or what we would like to consider as our heart's desire, only to find that the desire becomes a passing illusion that we fight hard to make reality or to get rid of while discovering that our desirable choices turned out to be misery for a moment.

Hmm, experience.

I was still sitting on the cold, beige, granular sand thinking as the light in my mind came on. The answer was plainly staring me right in the face sending me to the throne of grace. So I prayed and listened to my inner spirit providing the answer to my circumstance. Again, adding to my treasure, another valuable lesson.

Experience is the source that causes us to mature.
From experience we gain knowledge and a better understanding of ourselves. We then grow and develop wisdom. As long as we have life, we have something

juanita parker

to learn and something to pass along. Perhaps, when it's all said and done, it is a good thing to have experience.

Come Soothe My Soul

Dear Lord, thank you for being patient with my growth process. Thank you for assurance, comfort, strength and for today's experiences.

Assurance

When I think about life-threatening situations, I know it is a good thing to be centered in God.

For my own peace of mind, I reflect on the goodness of the Lord. Reflecting causes me to be thankful and grateful for God's mercy, grace and faithfulness towards me.

My trust in God allows me to stand firm in the assurance that I am never alone for his angels watch over me day and night. My heavenly Father loves me, protects me, and heals me.

Dear Father, I worship you, I give you praise and honor. You are my omnipotent Father, the almighty invincible God. You are all power, thank you for living great in my heart. Thank you for security in my spirit and blessed assurance in you. I will bless you at all times, most worthy Father.

juanita parker

Vision

Sitting in darkness, searching for light
Facing the shadows, what's wrong, what's right
Sin creates confusion
Fogs the mind, clouds the sight

Sitting in darkness, searching for light
A twinkle, a flash to open the mind
Guiding light, healing light
suddenly, it's clear!
No blurs of distortion
A change prevails
No longer destruction
Vision appears
A plan, a guide
The path is clear

Light in darkness, rest assured
Shines gloriously brighter
When vision's restored

Thank you Lord for opening our eyes, healing our spirits and focusing the light of our vision towards purpose.

juanita parker

The High Road

there are many roads traveled in life
at different intervals you may think that you are
wasting time through the struggle and fight
the important thing is to keep moving forward
for everything learned on the path has its purpose
as you seek to do all that you can
and to be all you can be
always remember you are a child of the King

never forget the positives that have been developed in you from within
stir up hope
relax with patience
use progressive action toward your aspirations and dreams
permit the forces of your spirit to keep working diligently
should idleness and stagnation cross your path at any time
embrace the wisdom of God
His force is so powerful
the strongest of iron doors will either break or open
for you optimistic adventurer, intelligent and gifted one

be persuaded to finish your mission with confidence
blaze a trail and someone will follow
perhaps to surpass all you have done
giving you the credit for inspiring them
to reach beyond the scope of their limits
so they too can be called innovative trailblazer
along with you, on the high road

Come Soothe My Soul

Thank you Lord for your amazing loving kindness. Thank you for keeping me as the apple of your eye. Thank you for permitting me to go beyond my expectations as I reach towards the higher ground that you have set for me. Let the presence of your Spirit encircle me, camp around me and guide me continuously. Thank you for help and favor. My desire is to complete the tasks I am assigned to for your glory. I put my trust in you. For this, I give you Praise – Blessed is the Lord my God forever. Hal-lelujah, Hallelujah, Amen, and Amen.

To correspond with author:
write to
Inspiration Plus, Communications
P.O. Box 35513
Los Angeles, CA 90035

Printed in the United States
16981LVS00003B/274-369